Special *Edition*
ILLUSTRATED

Andersonville

Penetrating views from men who were there
and from modern scholars

The following articles, first published in *Civil War Times Illustrated*,
are reissued in 1983 by Eastern Acorn Press—the publishing
imprint of Eastern National Park & Monument Association —with
permission of the original publisher and copyright holder, Historical
Times, Inc., Box 1831, Harrisburg, PA 17105: "A Guard at
Andersonville" © 1964, "The Andersonville Raiders" © 1971,
"Clerk of the Dead" © 1971, "The First War Crimes Trial" ("After
Andersonville") © 1976, "Patronize an Old Vet" ©1976.

Eastern National promotes and aids historic, scientific, and
educational activities of the National Park Service. As a nonprofit
cooperating association authorized by Congress, it makes
interpretive material available to park visitors by sale or free
distribution. It also supports research, interpretation, and
conservation programs of the Service.

COVER: North view of Andersonville Prison, showing Captain Wirz on
horseback taking a prisoner to stocks. The original drawing by John B.
Walder (Co. G, 141st Pa.) was lithographed by Anton Hohenstein and
published by T. Sinclair's in 1865. (LC) Design: Paul Bacon. OTHER
ILLUSTRATIONS: Sources are abbreviated as BL (*Battles and Leaders of
the Civil War*), LC (Library of Congress), HW (*Harper's Weekly*), FL
(*Frank Leslie's Illustrated Newspaper*), KA (Kean Archives), and NA
(National Archives).

PRODUCED BY THE PUBLISHING CENTER FOR CULTURAL RESOURCES. MANUFACTURED IN THE UNITED STATES OF AMERICA.

EASTERN   ACORN   PRESS

Recollections of a young Confederate officer
by JAMES DUNWODY JONES

[Editorial notes are in brackets.]

A north view of Andersonville Prison shows Captain Wirz on horseback taking a prisoner to stocks. The original drawing by John B. Walder (Co. G, 141st Pa.) was lithographed by Anton Hohenstein and published by T. Sinclair's in 1865. (LC)

A Guard at Andersonville

James Dunwody Jones, *born on a plantation in McIntosh County, Georgia, enlisted in the 8th Georgia Regiment at the age of 17. A skilled marksman, he distinguished himself at First Manassas, and won a battlefield promotion to lieutenant. At the end of the war he was a major. He wrote his memoirs some years after the war, and dedicated them with affection to his black servant Sim. Sim was with him during the four years of campaigning, nursed him to health each of the four times he was wounded, and at the end of the war went back with him to the plantation. The excerpt from his manuscript published here was furnished by Major Jones's daughter, Mrs. Mary J. Hillyer, New York.*

In 1864 I was ordered to duty with troops at the famous prison camp at Andersonville, Georgia, in the capacity of drillmaster and ordnance officer. No doubt you have heard many stories of Andersonville, some true, some false. Andersonville was no worse than Northern prisons. There was suffering at Andersonville; there was also suffering at Johnson's Island; there were hardships in all prisons. Thirty thousand men in a stockade are apt to suffer more or less.

The stockade consisted of about 16 to 20 acres with a 20-foot [actually 17-foot] wall of pine logs standing upright and embedded in the earth to a depth of 6 to 8 feet. The guards stationed on top of the wall overlooked the interior. The prisoners got fully as much, and as good rations as our guards. My servant Sim almost every day brought something from the cooks of the prison, who were paroled Federal soldiers, the cook house being outside the stockade. Sim often brought, from these cooks, ham, bacon, and beef for our use, when I could not draw a pound for myself from the quartermaster. And may I ask, whose fault was it that there was no exchange of prisoners? We would gladly have given 10 for 1 (and we had them to give) but no! The policy of the Federal government was to exhaust the South. That was General [U.S.] Grant's policy; and the only one that was a success.

While at Andersonville I witnessed the hanging of six Federal prisoners by the prisoners inside the stockade, an action for which Captain [Henry] Wirz should have been held blameless. The executed men were robbers and murderers of their fellow captives, and were on the eve of being lynched by the latter when Captain Wirz went in at the risk of his life and the lives of the men with him, rescued the accused, and placed them under guard outside the stockade. But this was only a compromise. The feeling against the accused was so bitter that the other prisoners said, "We will tear down the walls and come out and get them." Captain Wirz knew that they could do it, for the Confederate guards were undisciplined boys and old men.

One of my duties was inspection of guards. I found that of the 500 muskets carried by men going on sentry duty, not over 100 could have been fired. I had spoken to Captain Wirz of the inefficiency of the guard; consequently he knew he could not depend on them in case of a revolt of the prisoners.

So he was forced to make an agreement with the prisoners, as follows: Captain Wirz would continue in charge of the robbers until they were called for trial, they to be tried by a judge and jury selected from within the stockade, and under the laws of Georgia. If the accused were acquitted, Wirz was to send them to another prison camp. If they were convicted, he was to turn them over to the other prisoners for execution. Wirz also furnished one of the bastions of the stockade as a court room and placed Georgia law books at the disposal of the court. Lawyers from among the prisoners were selected to serve the prosecution and defense.

Court was opened, and jurors were drawn. Each accused was tried, and as there were quite a number, the trial lasted [about ten days]. Six were found guilty of murder and condemned to death by hanging.

Demand was made on Captain Wirz for the six guilty men. Where the prisoners got the lumber to build the gallows, or the rope for the executioner, I know not, as Wirz refused to furnish anything of the kind. [Jones is in error. Captain Wirz provided lumber for the scaffold.] Fulfilling his promise, on execution day he marched the condemned men under a separate guard into the stockade. I was one of the few who obtained a pass to occupy a sentry box to witness the executions, and I was quite near the scaffold. I will never forget that sea of upturned faces, nor the old captain on his gray horse, speaking in his broken English, saying, "Men, according to de promise what I make, I turn ober dese mens to you. But I beg you to giff me de life ob dese mens, and I will mofe dem where you nevvar see dem no more."

Twenty thousand voices shouted, "No! No!"

Wirz exclaimed, "You say no! Den Gott haf mercy on dere souls." He wheeled his horse and marched the guard out.

In a second hundreds of hands laid hold of the unfortunates and tied their hands behind them. [A group of Regulators, headed by "Limber Jim," took hold of and bound the six.] One by one they were forced up the ladder and on to the trap. As they started to tie one of the men, a big Irishman [Charles Curtis], a most splendid physical specimen, made one bound forward. His fists shot out like catapults, and a man went down with each blow. He sprang forward with the vain hope of escape. The vast crowd opened before his headlong charge, forming a lane through which he ran the gauntlet. On each side men struck at him as he passed, beating him with their sticks. It looked as if there were ten thousand rimless wheels turning in the air, and all the poor fellow could do was hold up his arms on each side of his head as he ran, the yelling mob closing in behind him.

He ran around two sides of the stockade, then suddenly took refuge in a hole. They soon pulled him out and brought him back to the place of execution. They placed him on the trap with the others. The trap was sprung and the six men

Photograph of James Dunwody Jones taken when he was a nineteen-year-old major in the Confederate Army. (Mrs. Mary Jones Hillyer)

shot downward. Five hung suspended, but the sixth man's [William Collins] rope broke and he fell to earth. Fifty hands caught him before he could move. The rope was taken from his neck. A man climbed the post and knotted the ends together.

I shall never forget the poor fellow's prayers and pleadings for his life, but he happened to be the leader of the gang and there was no mercy shown him. They forced him up the ladder and he had to pass his five comrades who were still quivering and struggling in their death agonies. He was forced to his place at the end of the scaffold. The trap having fallen he had to walk across a single 3 x 4 scantling and stand trembling upon it while they tied the rope around his neck. Then he was shaken off, by the executioners rocking back and forth the support on which he stood. It was terrible to see the miserable wretch's efforts to keep his equilibrium, but at last he lost his balance and with a fearful cry plunged into space.

The sight was horrible, but remember this was but justice meted out to six murderers by their fellow prisoners. The six are buried to one side in the National Cemetery at Andersonville. Seventeen thousand [13,700] other Federals are buried in this cemetery.

Captain Wirz could not have prevented the execution — that would have required 5,000 well-armed troops, who would have had to rescue the men by force and held the stockade in check.

About this time the great [George] Stoneman raid [July 27–30, 1864] for the relief of the Andersonville prisoners took place. It came so near succeeding that it [following General W. T. Sherman's September 2 capture of Atlanta] caused the transfer of the prisoners to South Carolina [and Georgia]. I had the pleasure and the honor of helping capture the Stoneman command.

Soon after the above event I was ordered to Columbia, South Carolina for assignment to command the interior of a stockade containing 1,250 Federal officers. To me this was one of the most pleasant episodes of the war. I soon made fast friends, I believe, of every officer in the prison, for it has always been my rule never to strike a fallen foe.

I always told the boys, "It is your privilege to try to get away, just as it is my business to keep you." I never punished a man for trying to escape.

The end of the war was drawing near, a fact we could not realize. Nevertheless it was quite patent. The officers from Illinois made me a most unheard-of and generous offer as a mark of their esteem and good will — a farm and stock, with provisions for one year, if I would go home with them when we were exchanged. Arrangements were already pending. They said, "You are bound to lose your Negroes and perhaps all your other property."

I could but thank the boys who meant so kindly toward me, and replied, "Gentlemen, we are friends now and you esteem me in my present relations toward you. But should I accept your generous offer, made in grateful kindness, what would be our relations when settled in our Western home? I would be pointed out as a deserter, a renegade, a coward, a man not to be trusted. I would be considered a man who failed like a craven to face the inevitable, and proved faithless to his country at the time of its greatest need. No, no, gentlemen, I thank you, but I must sink or swim with the ship."

They saw I was right, and said, "Forgive us, we only thought to save you from loss."

Then came the boom of Sherman's guns from across the Congaree River, and the hurried move of the prisoners by railroad to a safer place. A good many Yankees escaped during the evacuation of the prison, but we had no time to look for them. Among the escapees was a Captain Carpenter of Philadelphia, a fine gentleman. Also a Lieutenant Richardson of Boston, also a nice fellow. But he was not so fortunate as the others, for just as the train was about to pull out, a sallow-faced South Carolina boy armed with a shotgun came up and said to me, "Cap'n, I'se fotched a durn Yankee in; what shil I do wid him?"

The lieutenant was so covered with dirt I did not recognize him. Thinking it was one of Sherman's men, I replied, "Well, damn it, shoot him."

Quick as a flash the little cracker brought his gun down on Richardson, when the latter exclaimed, "My God! Don't tell him that, for it has been all I could do for that last two hours to keep him from shooting me. Don't you know me? I am Lieutenant Richardson."

"By George, old fellow," I answered. "I would never have known you, and the fact is, I don't know what to do with you. I have no place to put you, the cars are all closed, and as you can see, the train has started to move. I guess you had better go on to Sherman, as you had started that way."

Said he: "For God's sake, take me along. Don't leave me here."

"Well," I said, "give me your parole of honor. You can go back to the last car and jump on if you can. You will find my boy Sim there. Tell him I sent you, and that he is to take good care of you until I see you again."

I was on duty for three nights and two days without one moment's sleep or rest, and did not see Richardson the whole time, as my servant brought food to me on top of the cars. But Richardson got through all right and was exchanged shortly afterwards. Although I wrote to him several times I never received a reply.

A love affair came under my eye while I was at the Columbia prison camp. All prisoner correspondence came through my hands for inspection, and when it did not conflict with orders or the good of the Southern cause, I let it pass into the prison — most of it was so passed. One of the inmates was a captain whose name I will withhold, as he was an estimable gentleman. In the North before the war he had met a young woman, a great beauty of Columbia, South Carolina. When the fortunes of war brought him to that place as a prisoner, he renewed his acquaintanceship by mail, the letters being read by me as they passed. This friendly correspondence soon ripened the young man's feelings into love, and the couple became engaged. I even allowed her to send him her picture to cheer his lonely hours, and came very near getting into trouble over this. In some way the commanding officer learned that I had allowed a picture to go into the stockade. He became very angry over this, and ordered me to retrieve the picture and return it to the girl.

With some difficulty I obtained the picture from the captain and returned it to the lady, remarking, "You may give me that picture if you wish." She did so, and shortly afterwards I gave it to the captain, warning him to keep it to himself. I could not see how the possession of such an article could injure our cause, and it gave much comfort to a poor, lovesick prisoner.

The young woman's mother was a Northerner, a widow named Feaster, who had married a South Carolinian named Boozer. The girl, Mary, took the name of her stepfather, or at least was known locally as Mary Boozer. She was extremely beautiful, and the Yankee captain was deeply in love with her. He became one of my escapees, joined Sherman when the latter's army came through on its way north, and carried Mary Boozer along as his wife.

Like many wartime romances, however, the course of true love did not run smooth. Soon there was a divorce. Mary Boozer, as depraved as she was beautiful, drifted to New York and from there to Paris, where she trapped a wealthy Brazilian. She spent his money so freely that she soon had the old fool reduced to beggary. He blew out his brains.

Then she caught a French count, squandered his fortune, and got rid of him. The Siamese ambassador attached her to his suite and took her to Siam. But the ambassador did not have sufficient power to keep her from the interested eye of the Viceroy.

Soon Mary was installed in the Viceroy's harem, and her position was that of the favorite. Success seemed assured. Then she slipped. She took up with a French naval officer whose ship was in port. The old Viceroy, who was not at all broadminded, had her beautiful head removed by the executioner's sword.

Mary Boozer was not the first girl to lose her head over a sailor. Nor the last.

The horrors nine captives suffered
at the hands of fellow prisoners
reviewed by DAVID L. MALLINSON

Wartime photograph of Andersonville Prison stockade. (NA)

The Andersonville Raiders

Andersonville was hastily built when it became apparent that large numbers of prisoners were a military hazard in Richmond as well as a drain on the local food supply. Properly named Camp Sumter, it was northeast of Americus, Georgia. The prison consisted of a log stockade of 16½ acres, later enlarged to 26 acres; a sluggish stream ran through it. The disease and death rates were enormously high, with poor sanitation, crowding, exposure, and inadequate diet contributing to the unhealthful conditions. Only enlisted men were confined there, and in the summer of 1864 the number of prisoners at Andersonville totaled 32,899.

But perhaps worse than all other hardships the prisoners suffered, was the problem of the "Andersonville Raiders."

From the time a prisoner arrived at Andersonville, he was continually troubled by bullies, thieves, and murderers. These misfits came to be known as the "Andersonville Raiders" and they contributed heavily to the hardships of the other prisoners. The Raiders terrorized the stockade until they became the most dreaded horror of prison life.

The first Raiders were merely a small number of petty criminals who had been attracted to military service by the rewards of bounty-jumping and had been captured before they could collect their bounties and find an opportunity to desert. Other prisoners made their acquaintance at Belle Isle, Virginia, where they had been imprisoned before their removal to Andersonville. These recruits from the underworld grew into a formidable force of ruffians which eventually numbered between four and five hundred. The imprisonment of other criminal types swelled the Raiders' ranks, as did the degeneration of formerly upright men who succumbed to the temptation to partake of the fruits of robbery.

The Raiders formed themselves into bands numbering from five to twenty-five, each led by a bold, unscrupulous scoundrel. Among these leaders were Charles Curtis, 5th Rhode Island Artillery, John Sarsfield, 144th New York, Patrick Delaney, 83d Pennsylvania, and William Collins, 88th Pennsylvania. The followers of each were designated by the leader's name, as "Collins' Raiders" or "Curtis' Raiders." Collins was also called "Mosby" and his followers "Mosby's Raiders" after the famous Confederate Ranger, John S. Mosby. Sergeant John L. Ransom, of the 9th Michigan Cavalry, wrote in his diary on March 28, 1864: "Capt. Moseby, of the raiders, is in the same squad with me. He is quite an intelligent fellow and often talks with us. We lend him our boiling cup which he returns with thanks. Better to keep on the right side of him, if we can without countenancing his murderous operations."

At first the Raiders were content with petty thievery, which they carried out at night. But their boldness increased as they grew stronger and better disciplined. Sergeant Ransom wrote in his diary on April 28: "Raiders do about as they please, and their crimes would fill more paper than I have at my disposal."

Prison authorities did nothing to stop the Raiders and the other prisoners had no way of dealing with the problem.

New prisoners with good clothes, blankets, jewelry, and money were the favorite prey of the thieves. John W. Northrop wrote in his diary on May 25, the day after his arrival at Andersonville:

> The cry of 'raiders' awoke us last night & we remembered what we had been told by some of the old prisoners yesterday, about thieves—a set of brutal men who steal everything possible, & even robbed men of money & watches & in some cases brutally beating men so they die from the cause. They boldly take blankets from over men's heads standing over them with clubs, threatening to kill them if they move. They are regularly organized bandit bands led by the most desperate characters. Here they bear the name of Raiders. Going among the men of our Company we find they had not fully realized this unexpected danger & some had lost boots, knapsacks containing all they have, blankets, canteens, dishes, their small stock of provisions &c. In other parts we hear of pocket picking, assaults with clubs & this is the work of every night especially after new arrivals.

The Raiders were on the prowl in the prison looking for victims all the time, often attacking a tent and taking all its occupants' possessions, including the clothes off their backs. The advantage of organization was demonstrated when other prisoners came to the aid of the victims. On May 10, Sergeant Ransom wrote: "Occasionally a party of new comers stick together and whip the raiders, who afterward rally their forces and the affair ends with the robbers victorious. Stones, clubs, knives, sling shots, etc., are used on these occasions...."

The Raiders constantly improved their system. After they had carefully selected a victim, they would seize his possessions, club any friends who tried to assist him, and flee. Ransom noted: "Raiders getting more bold as the situation grows worse. Often rob a man now of all he has, in public, making no attempt at concealment."

The Raiders began to pounce on new prisoners as soon as they were fairly within the gate. About two thousand of those who arrived in early May provided excellent picking for the robbers. Captured at the siege of Plymouth, North Carolina, they had just received their veteran bounties and would have been sailing for home had they not been attacked and taken prisoner. Dressed in new uniforms and carrying well-filled knapsacks the "Plymouth Pilgrims" had in their possession large sums of money when they reached Andersonville. It was estimated that they were carrying between $25,000 and $100,000. Even those who had no money were still a bonanza to any Raiders who could succeed in plundering him. His watch and chain, shoes, knife, ring, handkerchief, combs, and other trifles would net several hundred dollars in Confederate money. Kindly appearing men would offer to show the newcomers where they could sleep, then during the night they would come back and rob them. If the victim resisted, he might have his throat slashed or his skull crushed.

The following entries from Sergeant Ransom's diary show the horrors which he witnessed as the orgy of plunder and violence increased. On May 25 he wrote: "Man killed by the raiders near where we slept. Head all pounded to pieces with a club. Murders an every day occurrence." On June 15: "Raiders now do just as they please, kill, plunder and steal in broad day light, with no one to molest them." On June 17: "Saw a new comer pounded to a jelly by the raiders. His cries for relief were awful, but none came. Must a few villains live at the expense of so many? God help us from these worse than Rebels." On June 25: "Raiders kill some one now every day. No restraint in the least. Men who were no doubt respectable at home, are now the worst villains in the world. One of them was sneaking about our quarters during the night, and Sanders knocked him about ten feet with a board. Some one of us must keep awake all the time, and on the watch, fearing to lose what little we have." Two days later: "Raiders going on worse than ever before. A perfect pandemonium. Something must be done, and that quickly. There is danger enough from disease, without being killed by raiders. Any moment fifty or a hundred of them are liable to pounce upon our mess, knock right and left and take the very clothing off our backs. No one is safe from them. It is hoped that the more peaceable sort will rise in their might and put them down."

June 29 marked the beginning of the end of the Raiders' reign of terror in the stockade. Several prisoners went to the

The South Gate, a main entrance to the inner stockade, with a guard house on the right and a sentry tower on each side. (Century Magazine)

gate and Captain Henry Wirz heard their pleas for help. Wirz told them that if they could point out the thieves "he would clear the Stockade of every son of a b----."

Prisoners directed guards to the dens of known Raiders. The guards seized them a few at a time, took them out, and returned for more. When they were confronted by men with guns the Raiders were meek, but when other prisoners attempted to take them without assistance from the guards they resisted vigorously.

While some prisoners were helping to locate the raiders, others ransacked their quarters for stolen property. The hunt yielded a large quantity of blankets, clothing, money, watches, jewelry, and articles of all descriptions. One of the prisoners wrote in his diary that the searchers found "two stockings filled with greenbacks . . . one of watches, two gold, & other things." There were also some reports of discovering buried bodies and skeletons. The Raiders' tents were destroyed; and tent poles, cooking utensils, and other items of value were confiscated.

On June 30 General John H. Winder, who had been in command of Camp Sumter since June 17, issued the following:

General Orders
No. 57

Camp Sumter,
Andersonville, Ga., June 30, 1864

I. A gang of evil-disposed persons among the prisoners of war at this post having banded themselves together for the purpose of assaulting, murdering, and robbing their fellow prisoners and having already committed all these deeds, it becomes necessary to adopt measures to protect the lives and property of the prisoners against the acts of these men, and, in order that this may be accomplished, the well-disposed prisoners may and they are authorized to establish a court among themselves for the trial and punishment of all such offenders.

II. On such trials the charges will be distinctly made with specifications setting forth the time and place, a copy of which will be furnished the accused.

III. The whole proceedings will be properly kept in writing, all the testimony fairly written out as nearly in the words of the witnesses as possible.

IV. The proceedings, findings, and sentence in each case will be sent to the commanding officer for record, and if found in order and proper, the sentence will be ordered by execution.

By order of Brig. Gen. John H. Winder:

W.S. Winder,
Assistant Adjutant General

The next step was the judgment and punishment of the arrested ones. There were about 125 of the most noted Raiders under arrest. Captain Wirz had all sergeants of detachments assembled and he selected twenty-four of them to serve as jurors. For each trial twelve jurymen were chosen by lot.

The court was made up of prisoners themselves and from these prisoners were picked the judge and counsel. It was

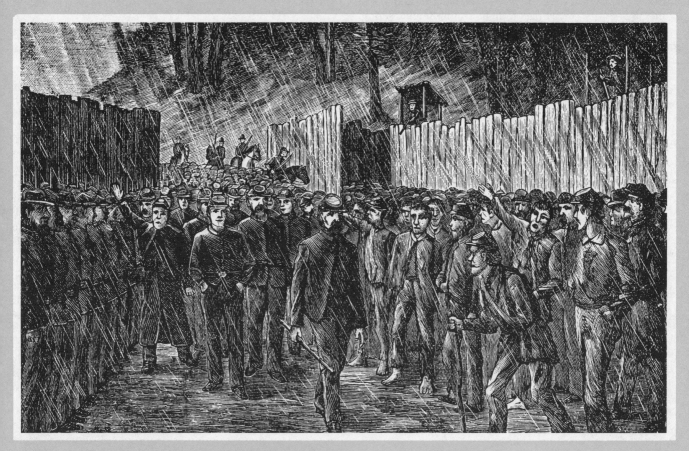

Prisoners entering Andersonville Prison. (Battlefield and Prison Pen)

probably a fair trial and the Raiders received a defense, but this did them no good.

Six of the Raiders were sentenced to be hanged, and many of the others were condemned to lighter punishment: sitting in the stocks, being strung up by their thumbs, or running the gantlet, and a few were forced to wear ball and chain. The court had been severe, but just.

The six who were found guilty of murder and sentenced to death by hanging were: Charles Curtis, 5th Rhode Island Artillery; John Sarsfield, 144th New York; Patrick Delaney, 83d Pennsylvania; William Collins, alias Mosby, 88th Pennsylvania; A. Munn, United States Navy; and Cary Sullivan, 72d New York. On Sullivan's headstone at Andersonville National Cemetery appears the inscription: "W. Rickson, U.S.N."

The executions were approved by General Winder and on Sunday evening, July 10, Father Peter Whelan, a Catholic priest, visited the condemned men. Five of them were Catholics and received the consolations of their religion from the priest.

On July 11, lumber was brought into the prison by the Rebels, and a gallows was erected for the purpose of executing the six condemned Raiders. A group of prisoners formed a square around the workers to keep the crowd from interfering and to avoid theft of the lumber. Some of the prisoners expected that an attempt would be made by friends of the condemned to destroy the scaffold and release them.

About 4:30 p.m., the six condemned Raiders were brought inside by Captain Wirz and some guards, and delivered over to the prison police force.

Accompanying Captain Wirz was Father Whelan, who remembered a short speech that Wirz addressed to the prisoners. The speech went something like this: "Boys, I have taken these men out and now I return them to you, having taken good care of them. I now commit them to you. You can do with them as you see fit." Then turning around to the condemned men he said, "May the Lord have mercy on your souls."

After Wirz made his speech, he withdrew his guards and left the condemned at the mercy of the remaining 28,000 enraged prisoners who had all been wronged by these men. Their hands were tied behind them, and one by one they mounted the scaffold. Curtis managed to get his hands loose and broke away. He ran through the crowd and down toward the swamp. Reaching the swamp, he plunged in, trying to get to the other side, where presumably were his friends. Half way across the swamp he collapsed and could go no farther.

The police started after him, waded in, and helped him out. He pled for some water and it was given to him. Then he was led back to the scaffold and helped to mount it.

The condemned men asked Father Whelan to appeal to their fellow prisoners to spare them. He did so, but he was unable to persuade them.

Each of the condemned men was given a chance to make a final speech. Sullivan had nothing to say. Munn said he came into the prison four months earlier perfectly honest, but starvation and evil companions had made him what he was. He also spoke of his mother and sisters in New York, and that he cared nothing as far as he himself was concerned, but the news that would be carried home to his family made him want to curse God he had ever been born.

Delaney said that he would rather be hanged than live the way most of the prisoners had to live on their allowance of rations. If allowed to steal he said he could get enough to eat, but as that was stopped he would rather be dead. He bid all good-bye. Said his name was not Delaney and that no one knew who he really was, therefore his family and friends would never know his fate; his Andersonville history would die with him.

Curtis said he didn't care a damn. He just wanted to get it over with, and not make such a fuss over a very small matter. Collins said he was innocent of murder and should not be hanged. He asked to be spared for the sake of his wife and child. Sarsfield, like Munn, blamed evil associates for bringing him to this end.

After the speeches were concluded the executioners pulled a meal sack over the head of each doomed man and fixed the nooses while Father Whelan prayed aloud.

About 5 o'clock the six condemned had their hands and feet tied, the nooses were adjusted and the plank was knocked from under them. Collins' rope broke and he fell to the ground, with blood spurting from his ears, mouth, and nose. As he was being lifted back to the scaffold he revived and begged fruitlessly for his life. He was soon dangling with the rest, and he died very hard. Munn and Delaney both died easily, but all the rest went slowly, particularly Sarsfield, who drew his knees nearly to his chin and then straightened them out with a jerk, the veins in his neck swelling as if they would burst.

After hanging for about fifteen minutes the six bodies were taken down and carried outside. The crowd dispersed quietly. Although minor crimes continued, offenders were thereafter punished by the prison police force, which was able to maintain a reasonable degree of order in the stockade after the hangings. The "Andersonville Raiders" were no more.

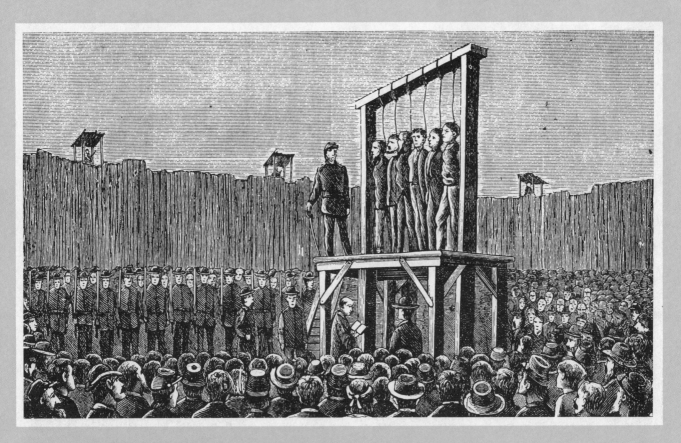

Hanging of the Raiders in Andersonville Prison. (Battlefield and Prison Pen)

The story of Dorence Atwater's battle
to identify the Andersonville casualities
retraced by TERRY E. BALDWIN

Burying the dead at Andersonville, summer of 1864. The dead were interred side by side, without coffins, in trenches four feet deep. (Photographic History of the Civil War)

Clerk of the Dead

An old Civil War cannon stands on the northeast end of Baldwin Park in Terryville, Connecticut, as a tribute to the memory of Dorence Atwater, a soldier in the Connecticut Volunteers. Captured and taken to Andersonville Prison, Atwater secretly compiled a list of the names of 12,920 dead soldiers there. Moreover, after his release from Andersonville, he personally contended with the War Department of the United States Government for the publicizing of that list, and was ultimately successful.

Dorence Atwater, the son of Henry and Catherine Fenn Atwater, was born in Terryville, Connecticut, on February 3, 1845. His education consisted of meager public schooling, but this farm boy did manage to develop a flair for penmanship. When the Civil War broke out, he was clerking in the village store. Being of large stature, Atwater easily passed for 18, though he was only 16. He had the true spirit of patriotism and, unknown to his parents, enlisted on August 19, 1861, in the First Squadron Connecticut Cavalry.

When Atwater left Connecticut, his unit was transferred to the Harris Light Cavalry, the 2d New York, commanded by the colorful I. Judson Kilpatrick. He participated in the hard campaigning and sharp battles that command experienced, and after nearly two years of service, while carrying dispatches near Hagerstown, Maryland, on July 7, 1863, he was captured by two Rebel scouts dressed in Union uniforms.

Atwater was first sent to Belle Isle on the James River, where he remained for five months. Through the intervention of a friend he was transferred to Richmond, and forced to walk barefooted across the city on a bleak December day. At Smith's tobacco factory in Richmond, he was put in charge of the supplies which were sent from the North to be distributed to Federal prisoners. It is interesting to note that he found one of the Confederate officers purloining the goods, and was instrumental in getting him discharged.

A new Southern prison at Andersonville, Georgia, had just been opened in the early months of 1864. Four hundred prisoners were being taken each day from Belle Isle to that prison. They were brought through Richmond, and if for any reason the full quota did not number 400 when it reached the city, more prisoners were added to supply the full allotment. Thus one night Atwater found himself unceremoniously routed out of bed to be taken to Andersonville.

At the time of Atwater's arrival there on March 23, 1864, Union prisoners were dying at the rate of 130 a week. Suffering from chronic diarrhea since his capture, he was confined in the stockade until May 18, when he was sent to the prison hospital. His health improved, and on June 15 he was paroled and detailed as a clerk in the office of the surgeon, Isaiah H. White, to keep the daily records of death of Federal prisoners of war at Andersonville, and to make monthly and quarterly abstracts of the deaths.

Atwater was informed that when the war was over, the list would be exchanged with the Union Government. He undertook the work and was allowed outside the stockade during the day, but confined inside during the night. His desk was next to that of Captain Henry Wirz, which enabled Atwater to observe the casual way business was conducted. He deduced that the death register would never be preserved, and so in the latter part of August he began secretly copying the roll of Union dead.

Atwater's method of keeping the death register was to take from the board or post over each grave the number he had placed there as the bodies were laid side by side in long trenches. The name, number, state, unit, date of death, and disease were reported. This is illustrated in the following authentic example which was taken from his completed list:

Number of grave, 2,380; name, Anderson, A.; regiment, 14th Cavalry, Co. K; died, June 23; disease diarrhea.

Atwater succeeded in recording the names of 12,920 dead soldiers. He kept his secret copy in his coat lining until he had safely passed through the lines in March 1865. Dorence arrived at Camp Parole in Annapolis, Maryland on March 12, but found that he could not get a furlough because his term of service had expired some seven months before. This delay was exasperating to Atwater; he was anxious to get a leave of absence for thirty days in order to have his "death register" published for the relief of the many thousands of anxious relatives and friends. He wrote to Secretary of War Edwin M. Stanton, but before a reply could be returned, the commandant of the camp granted him a furlough. Atwater went directly to his home in Terryville, where he was confined for three weeks with a serious attack of diphtheria. Like so many Civil War veterans, Dorence Atwater had gone to war a strong, robust boy, but returned a sickly skeleton.

On April 12, 1865, Atwater received a telegram from the War Department requesting him to come to Washington and bring his rolls. If they were found acceptable, the telegram implied that he would be suitably rewarded. Despite his illness, he boarded a train for Washington. He arrived on the same night (April 14) that President Lincoln was assassinated.

Dorence presented himself to Major Samuel Breck early the next morning. Breck informed the former soldier that Secretary of War Stanton had authorized him to pay $300 for the rolls. Atwater stated that he did not wish to sell them, but that they ought to be published for the benefit of the relatives and friends of the dead, for whom they had been copied. Major Breck, obviously angered, told him that if he published the rolls, the War Department would call them contraband and confiscate them. Moreover, Atwater was given until nine o'clock the following morning to decide whether he would or would not take the $300.

In this close-up photograph of Andersonville prisoners, apparently taken from the top of the stockade, the men are receiving rations. (NA)

Thus threatened, Atwater realized that his rolls, which were already in Breck's possession, would be taken from him, and so he replied: "Give me $300, a clerkship, and my rolls back again as soon as they are copied and you can take them."

Major Breck agreed to this, and shortly thereafter Atwater returned to Terryville to nurse his ailing father, who died on April 25, 1865. While at home he sent Major Breck a drawing of the Andersonville cemetery, and a letter stating how the dead were buried. Moreover, Atwater explained that if immediate measures were taken, the graves could be identified. He said that if the Government would furnish sufficient headboards, he would have them properly marked and erected.

In the latter part of May, Atwater telegraphed from New York asking Colonel Breck if his rolls had been copied, and he received a reply of "not yet." On June 1, he began his clerical duties in Washington and upon numerous occasions demanded the return of his rolls. Atwater wished to copy the rolls after business hours and ultimately to have them published for benefit of the friends of the deceased. Major Breck, after consulting with Adjutant General E.D. Townsend, stated that "the rolls shall not be copied for any traffic whatever."

Dorence Atwater in later life.

It is interesting to note that in the weeks after Dorence Atwater had passed through the lines in March 1865, the identity of the graves was brought to the attention of Secretary of War Edwin Stanton by Clara Barton, founder of the American Red Cross. She was convinced that Atwater's method of identifying the graves was a valid one, and urged Stanton to order an expedition to accomplish that goal. The request was granted, and as a result a Government-sponsored expedition set out for Andersonville, Georgia on July 8, 1865. It consisted of a party of thirty-four workmen, clerks, and letterers under the command of Captain James N. Moore, assistant quartermaster at Washington, and included Dorence Atwater and Clara Barton. The party reached its destination at noon July 25, and during the three weeks that followed a cemetery covering fifty square acres was enclosed. Moreover, with the assistance of additional men from the garrison at Macon, headboards were erected to mark a total of 12,920 graves. Of this number, the original register kept by Atwater, and seized at Andersonville by Major General James H. Wilson, furnished about 10,500 names. The remaining 2,000 names were supplied from a copy made by Dorence Atwater in the Andersonville prison and brought by him to Annapolis on his return with the paroled prisoners. The other 460 graves were marked by headboards reading "Unknown Union Soldier." As a result, Clara Barton, in her *Report to the People of the United States of America*, could announce that the expedition was highly successful, and tell all Americans that "for the record of your dead you are indebted to the forethought, courage, and perseverance of a nineteen-year-old soldier named Dorence Atwater."

Clara Barton, founder of the American Red Cross, collaborated with Atwater in laying out the National Cemetery at Andersonville and later fought for justice for Atwater. (LC)

A few days before the Andersonville-bound expedition departed from Washington, the original rolls were returned to Atwater in order that he supply the aforementioned deficiency of 2,000 names in the original register captured by General Wilson. Dorence now planned to retain a complete list of all the names included in his rolls and give it to the surviving relatives and friends of the Andersonville dead. Consequently, when the originals were needed in the Wirz trial at Washington, they and Atwater's copy were in his tent when the messenger arrived in Georgia to claim them. The messenger took the original, but left Dorence's copy in the latter's possession. When the grave-marking expedition left for home on August 17, Dorence placed his copy of the rolls in his trunk and brought it to Washington.

Upon his arrival, Atwater reported to Major Breck at the War Department. The latter asked Dorence if he knew where the copy of the rolls was, and the reply was: "I have it, will you allow me to keep the list now that you have had the names copied here?" Breck told Atwater that he could keep the rolls only if he paid back the $300 to the Government. Otherwise, all copies were to become the property of the War Department and Atwater was forbidden to publish them.

He refused to return his copy because he felt that the names should be published for the benefit of the public. Major Breck labeled this intended action as a "money-making venture," and ordered that Atwater's room and trunk be searched. When the rolls could not be found, Atwater was arrested and taken to Old Capitol Prison. In a few days he was arraigned and tried by court-martial on two charges. The first charge was based on his conduct to the prejudice of good order and military discipline. The second charge was larceny.

The court met on five different days, September 2, 4, 5, 7, 11, and found Dorence Atwater guilty of both charges. He was sentenced to dishonorable discharge from the United States service, a fine of $300, confinement at hard labor for a period of eighteen months, and was ordered to return the "stolen" property to the War Department.

The Secretary of War designated the state prison at Auburn, New York as the place of confinement. On September 26, 1865, Dorence arrived at Auburn State Prison, and began his sentence at hard labor. Almost at once powerful friends, led by Clara Barton, Major General Benjamin F. Butler, Horace Greeley, and many other notable men and women of the time, began to work in his behalf. As a result, Dorence Atwater, after serving more than two months at hard labor, was discharged by order of Secretary Stanton and became the first man, according to future United States Senator Orville H. Platt, to leave Auburn Prison without a discharge order by the court or an executive pardon. (Later

President Andrew Johnson did give him a general pardon.)

Although a free man, Dorence Atwater had been deeply humiliated and disgraced. Penniless and in poor health, he reached New Haven, Connecticut, on the day after his release, and learned that the record had not yet been furnished to the surviving relatives and friends. Immediately he turned to Horace Greeley, editor of the New York *Tribune*, who enthusiastically agreed to publish a book containing Atwater's Andersonville prison records. Within forty days, Dorence had the list ready for the Tribune Publishing Company.

While Greeley began his task, the stigma of the court-martial plagued Atwater. On July 11, 1867, the state of Connecticut honored the Civil War veteran by presenting him with a memorial for "courageous and patriotic service to the United States of America." Yet in spite of his Connecticut honor, Dorence was not officially pardoned, and he began to consider living in voluntary exile from the land which mistreated him. President Andrew Johnson, urged by Clara Barton, rewarded him for his graves identification work by making him a U.S. consul. In 1868, he was sent to the Seychelles Islands in the Indian Ocean.

Meanwhile, to the surprise of the War Department, the New York *Tribune's* book appeared on the news stands. Eager readers snatched up the copies as soon as they rolled from the presses. The Death Register sold at twenty-five cents per copy, barely covering the cost of printing. It furnished invaluable information to the friends and relatives of the soldiers of the North.

Shortly after Atwater took up his duties in the Seychelles Islands, the consulate was suspended, but he was transferred to Tahiti in the Society Islands in 1871 by President Ulysses S. Grant. He was reluctant to leave the Seychelles Islands, but rehabilitated himself in beautiful Tahiti, soon winning the love and admiration of the natives. They referred to him as "Tupuatooroa," which means "wise man." Atwater courted Moetia Salmon, a native princess of great beauty, whose father was an English gentleman in business for many years in Tahiti. Dorence married her in 1875, and in a short time he had learned the Tahitian legends, tribal relations, and family trees better than most of the natives.

His innate ingenuity did not fail him for long in Tahiti. Trade and speculation brought him gold, and soon Atwater organized an expedition for pearls. It was a highly successful venture, and the once-impoverished Dorence Atwater became a recognized pearl king as well as a member of Tahitian royalty. It was then that Robert Louis Stevenson met and wrote about him in *Ebb Tide*. They became very good friends, and together founded the first steamship line from Tahiti to San Francisco, a line which Atwater continued to own and control personally to the day of his death.

Secretary of War Edwin McM. Stanton consigned Atwater to the state prison at Auburn, N.Y., when a court-martial found him guilty of breach of discipline and larceny. (NA)

Robert Louis Stevenson (right) in Tahiti, where Atwater met him and became his close friend. (Scribner's Magazine)

While Dorence Atwater was living in Tahiti, Clara Barton and Atwater's brother Francis, a New Haven publisher and later a Connecticut senator, were continually trying to clear his name. In 1895, the aged woman of Red Cross fame appeared before the townspeople of Terryville and delivered a stirring appeal. In her speech, Miss Barton urged that the town take action to purge the record of Dorence Atwater and to have his dishonorable discharge from the army corrected. It produced a powerful effect and steps were taken by Connecticut senators and congressmen to have an honorable discharge for Atwater.

The desired action came in 1898, when the hated court martial verdict was set aside as a "great wrong." Thus the 33-year-old stain was finally removed from the Connecticut soldier's record. According to Brigadier General Joseph Hawley, it was the first instance then on record of Congress overruling the decision of a court-martial.

After the news of the honorable discharge reached Terryville, the trustees of Baldwin Park proposed to perpetuate the memory of Dorence Atwater. Judge Jason C. Fenn, a member of the committee, heard that one of the old Rodman cannons, now no longer used by the army, might be obtained to adorn the little park and at the same time mark a historical event. He spoke of it to his fellow committeemen and got their approval.

The Government readily donated the cannon, and it was brought from one of the forts in Boston Harbor to the knoll in Baldwin Park at a transportation cost of $175. The committee planned to build a granite base for the cannon, and to erect a metal table upon it. The tablet would recite briefly the special service of Atwater. Including the transportation fee, the memorial would cost the town approximately $600. Judge Fenn advanced the money required to bring the cannon to Terryville, and the remaining price was to be paid by private contributions.

An opposition group to the proposed Atwater Memorial appeared in the neighboring city of Bristol, when a meeting of the Gilbert W. Thompson Post, G.A.R., voted to disapprove the project. They pointed to Atwater's courtmartial, his dishonorable discharge, and his imprisonment for theft of a document from the Government. On the other hand, Atwater's friends contended that he merely stood upon his rights, and refused to give up what was clearly his own. Moreover, they stated that he performed a distinguished service for his countrymen, and that no other Terryville man had done so fine a service in connection with the Civil War. At the height of the dispute, Atwater's brother Richard, in an open letter to the G.A.R. post, challenged its members to meet him in public and take up the "derogatory charges and appalling ignorance of the facts."

The Gilbert W. Thompson Post avoided Richard Atwater's public challenge, and their opposition movement slowly

The Dorence Atwater Memorial in Baldwin Park, Terryville, Connecticut. (Terry E. Baldwin)

faded away. As a result, the Atwater memorial drive was ultimately successful, and a dedication held on Memorial Day, 1907 with Clara Barton present. In 1908, with his dusky princess wife, he visited Terryville and saw the memorial in his honor. The villagers flocked to Baldwin Park to catch a glimpse of this person of great fame who until that day had been a mystery to nearly all.

Weakened by years of continual sickness, Atwater went to San Francisco for medical treatment in 1910. He was ready to return to his Tahitian home when he suddenly became gravely ill and died in a hotel room on November 28.

Dorence Atwater's last wish was to be buried in Tahiti, and his body was made ready to ship back to his island home. On the San Francisco pier, an elaborate cortege was present to see him off on January 10, 1911. It included fifty veterans of the Lincoln Post, Grand Army of the Republic, who paid their final respects. In addition, a Presidential tribute was evoked in memory of the deceased U.S. consul.

Tahiti went into mourning when Atwater's body arrived for burial on January 22, 1911. Tribal pallbearers, trained to officiate only at royal funerals, escorted the body from the steamer on which it arrived to its final resting place at Papara, twenty-two miles away.

The Tahitians erected a simple granite monument in his memory, which included a reference to the inscription on the memorial in Terryville, but no mention of what he had done to mark the resting places of 12,920 other comrades in Blue.

Andersonville Prison occupying a bare twenty-six acres was enclosed by a double palisade made of pine logs. A railing inside the stockade constituted a "deadline"; anyone caught crossing it or threatening to do so was instantly shot. No shelter was furnished: men pooled their blankets and rigged them into tents with beanpoles which sold for $1.50 each. Water came from wells the prisoners dug with bare hands or with improvised tools and from the swamp which ran through the center of the stockade. The open latrines were along this small creek, and the sewage of the guard's camp, outside, also emptied into it. Flies and maggots swarmed over the entire area, accounting for a fatal dysentery which, along with scurvy, resulted in a death rate of up to 127 men daily. (NA)

The judgement and execution of Henry Wirz
recounted by ROBERT L. and KATHARINE M. MORSBERGER

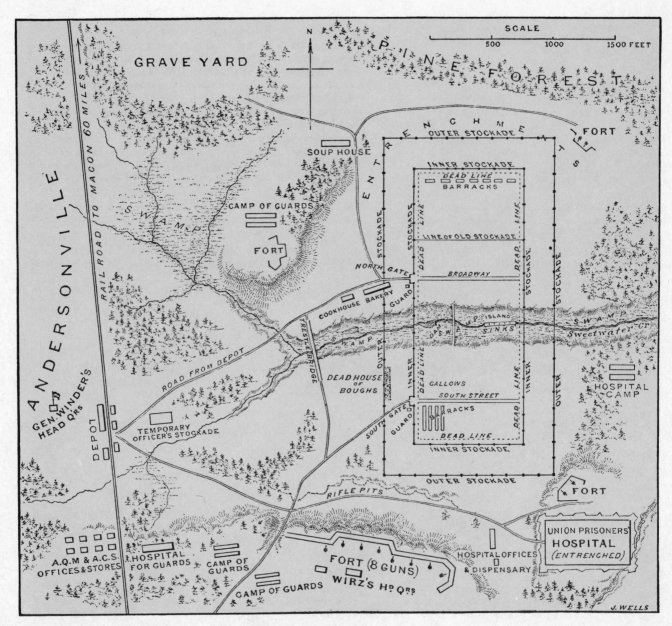

Plan of stockade and surroundings at Andersonville. (Century Magazine)

The First War Crimes Trial

As the Union prisoners of war found their way home in the late winter and early spring of 1865, stories began to circulate about the horrors of Confederate prison camps. Most of them were grim enough, but revelations about one swelled into a tale of unspeakable atrocity—Andersonville! There had been rumors of overcrowding, scurvy, and starvation, but no one was prepared for the sight of the survivors or for their tales of suffering. Walt Whitman wrote:

> I have seen a number of them. The sight is worse than any sight of battle-fields, or any collection of wounded, even the bloodiest. There was, (as a sample), one large boat load, of several hundreds, brought...to Annapolis; and out of the whole number only three individuals were able to walk from the boat. The rest were carried ashore and laid down in one place or another. Can those be *men*—those little livid brown, ash-streak'd, monkey-looking dwarfs?—are they really not mummied, dwindled corpses? They lay there, most of them, quite still, but with a horrible look in their eyes and skinny lips (often with not enough flesh on the lips to cover their teeth.) Probably no more appalling sight was ever seen on this earth. The dead there are not to be pitied as much as some of the living that come from there—if they can be call'd living—many of them are mentally imbecile, and will never recuperate.

These living skeletons were photographed and the pictures published in *Harper's Weekly* on June 17. Some Andersonville prisoners who had escaped or been exchanged earlier published their prison diaries or recollections of their torments, and others spread the story by word of mouth. These revelations incited a crescendo of outrage and a furious cry for revenge. "There are deeds, crimes that may be forgiven; but this is not among them," wrote Whitman. "It steeps its perpetrators in blackest, escapeless, endless damnation." Andersonville was an atrocity beyond the recognized horrors of warfare, and someone had to be held criminally responsible. The nation's need for vengeance focused on the prison's commandant, Captain Henry Wirz.

While the Confederate generals in the CIS-Mississippi were surrendering their forces, Wirz stayed on at Andersonville, apparently paralyzed by indecision. To Major General James H. Wilson, commanding Federal troops in the area, he explained that he was Swiss and planned to return to Europe. Wirz insisted that "The duties I had to perform were arduous and unpleasant, and I am satisfied that no man can or will justly blame me for things that happened here, and which were beyond my power to control.... Still I now bear the odium, and men who were prisoners have seemed disposed to wreak their vengeance upon me for what they have suffered—I, who was only the medium, or, I may better say, the tool in the hands of my superiors." Unmoved, Wilson had Wirz arrested on May 7. Two weeks later, Wirz was put on a train to Washington. Along the route, from Macon, Georgia, to Cincinnati, ex-prisoners tried to kill him at railroad stops. At Chattanooga and Nashville, there were such fierce assaults on Wirz's guards that at Louisville he was made to shave his beard and moustache and disguise himself in a black suit and beaver hat.

While Wirz languished in the Old Capitol Prison, Secretary of War Edwin M. Stanton directed Colonel Norton P. Chipman of the Judge Advocate's department to collect evidence for a trial. Chipman spent three months interviewing Andersonville prisoners and guards and locating witnesses. To head the military commission that would try Wirz, President Andrew Johnson appointed Major General Lew Wallace, probably on the strength of his performance at the Lincoln murder trial. Wallace was ordered to meet with the commission in Washington "on August 19, 1865, or as soon thereafter as practicable...." Serving under him were six generals and three colonels, including Chipman as prosecuting attorney of the commission. Wallace considered the commission to be "composed of able and well-disposed gentlemen."

As with the Lincoln conspirators murder trial, the Federal Government tried to implicate the leaders of the Confederacy. Wallace wrote to his wife on August 18, the day that he was appointed president of the commission, "I hear also that the prisoner's defense will be that he obeyed orders received from his superiors—in other words, it is expected that out of this investigation will come proof of Jeff. Davis connection with that criminality. *Quien Sabe!*"

The commission convened on August 21 in the Court of Claims room in the Capitol. Chipman's first indictment accused Wirz of conspiring with Jefferson Davis, Robert E. Lee, Confederate Secretary of War James Seddon, and others to inflict "wanton cruelty" upon Union prisoners with the intent of injuring their health and destroying their lives. A second charge of murder "in violation of the laws and customs of war" accused Wirz of thirteen specifications. Throughout, the charges accused Wirz not merely of negligence or incompetence but of having an evil, malicious, and cruel intent and with personally murdering numerous prisoners or ordering them to be killed, though in all cases their names were unknown.

Wirz accused the court of having predetermined his guilt, and Wallace wrote that day to his wife, "The prisoner is undoubtedly of opinion that he is in danger of some kind of punishment." Yet though Wallace claimed impartiality, his description of the prisoner seems to bear out Wirz's charge:

> Wirz is a singular looking genius. He has a small head; retreating forehead, high on the *os frontis* because the hair, light in colour, is very thin, threatening him with speedy baldness; prominent ears; small, sharp pointed nose, moustache and beard heavy enough to conceal the mouth and lower face, and of the dirty tobacco-stain colour; eyes large, and of mixed blue and grey, very restless, and of a peculiar transparency, remind-

ing one continually of a cat's when the animal is excited by the scent of prey; in manner he is nervous and fully alarmed, avoids your gaze, and withers and shrivels under the knit-brows of the crowd. His complexion is ashen and bloodless, almost blue. Altogether he was well chosen for his awful duty. . . .

Secretary of War Stanton personally read the charges on the opening day but became furious when he found Chipman's conspiracy charges couched in extravagant language similar to that which had embarrassed him in the Lincoln murder trial, charging Davis, Lee, and other high-ranking Confederates as accomplices. Stanton had the court adjourned, and the next morning Wallace announced that President Johnson had "dissolved" the commission so that a new indictment could be drawn up. It removed Davis and Lee and charged Wirz alone with direct and indirect murder. Several of Wirz's attorneys thereupon resigned, on grounds that a second indictment put the defendant in double jeopardy. Wirz shouted that without counsel he was being delivered to the hangman.

On August 23 the commission reconvened and the trial proper began, after Wirz pleaded "not guilty." Two of his attorneys remained as counsel for the defense—Otis H. Baker and Louis Schade. Besides the commissioners and the defense, there were reporters and spectators attending from curiosity. Wallace complained that "The investigation will oc-cupy at least two months—the hot, unwholesome, malarial months here by the Potomac."

The prosecution was conducted by Colonel Chipman, a 27-year-old Iowan who combined professional ambition with zealous hatred for the Confederacy. Otis Baker did most of the speaking for the defense, and the trial became a sort of duel between these antagonists. Wirz protested that he was protected from punishment by the terms of armistice, under which there was to be amnesty for Confederate soldiers and officers. He insisted that if anyone were responsible, it was his commanding officers in the prison system, Brigadier General John H. Winder and Major General Howell Cobb. He maintained that a Union military commission had no jurisdiction to try a Confederate officer and that he was not charged with any offense punishable under the laws of war, since he was merely following orders.

When Wirz protested that Captain Henry E. Noyes, who arrested him, broke his promise that Wirz should have safe conduct back to his home, Chipman countered that the agreement for surrender by rebel soldiers did not extend amnesty for "offences and crimes in violation of the laws of war" and that any violation of safe-conduct was irrelevant and had no bearing upon the court; that upon learning of the crimes at Andersonville, General Wilson had no power to absolve the prisoner and was justified in revoking the safe-conduct. Only a special pardon by the President could "give exemption from trial for actions in violation of the laws and customs of civilized warfare."

The Old Capitol Prison, Washington, where Wirz was confined. (NA)

Baker responded that Chipman had no right to assume Wirz guilty and that in any case he should be tried by a proper civilian tribunal. A military court could not hold subordinate officers as criminals for every killing committed under their command unless it was prepared to indict hundreds of thousands from both armies. Wallace overruled all of these objections and ordered the trial to proceed. Repeatedly Baker argued that his client would have certain rights in a civil court, only to have Chipman and Wallace reply that it was a military tribunal.

In 1865 military commissions operated under *Instructions for the Government of Armies of the United States in the Field*, prepared by Francis Lieber, a German emigré and veteran of Waterloo, who was professor of law and political science at Columbia University. In May 1863 Lincoln approved these as General Orders No. 100. Lieber wrote that warfare does not justify atrocities, that "Men who take up arms against one another in public war do not cease on this account to be moral beings, responsible to one another and to God." In 1865, the precedent was yet to be established, and a major issue in the trial was the jurisdiction of the court. Afterward, Judge Advocate General Joseph Holt wrote that a military trial left the court "unencumbered by the technicalities and inevitable embarrassments attending the administration of justice before civil tribunals."

Whatever the degree of Wirz's personal responsibility, the trial established beyond doubt the atrocity of Andersonville. One hundred and forty-eight witnesses—Union prisoners, Confederate guards, and prison doctors—all confirmed the basic conditions, until their testimony became a litany of horrors.

Andersonville is in southwestern Georgia, sixty miles from Macon. Toward the end of 1863 the Confederacy found that its already existing prisons were becoming unbearably overcrowded and that another would be necessary to relieve the strain. Andersonville was chosen as a site because it was farther from the front and easier to guard than prisons in Virginia. By February 1864 the prison stockade was nearly completed and named Camp Sumter. Originally, it enclosed sixteen and a half acres with a wall of rough-hewn pine logs seventeen feet high. A platform ran around the outside, three feet below the top of the wall, with sentry boxes first located at forty-yard intervals. Within, parallel with the stockade and making a circuit nineteen feet from it, was a dead line that prisoners were forbidden to cross. It consisted of posts six inches thick and about three feet high, with a strip of scantling nailed on top to form a rail. Anyone crossing it would be shot.

The stockade was designed for only 10,000 men, but by early May there were 12,000 prisoners; by mid-May, there were 19,000; by June 8, the list had risen to over 23,000 and on several days more than one hundred died. That month the north end of the stockade was enlarged by ten acres, but that was insufficient to relieve the congestion and the ranks of

Captain Henry Wirz, commandant at Andersonville Prison. (LC)

prisoners kept swelling until by August 9 there were over 33,000. Overcrowding was so severe that each man had less than four square yards. Every tree, except two, was felled by the prisoners for fuel, leaving the prisoners with no concealment but also with no shade. There were only rude hovels for the men, despite the fact that winter temperatures were occasionally below freezing, while summer heat could rise to well over 100. No clothing was provided, and the uniforms in which the men were captured soon became rags or ripped and rotted completely away, leaving some of the men naked to the elements.

The only water came from a small stream about a yard wide and a foot deep, flanked by a waist deep swamp extending about 150 feet on either side. This stream provided all the water for drinking, cooking, washing, and latrine purposes. Into it was thrown all the grease and garbage from the cook house as well as the prisoners' excrement. Dr. Joseph Jones, a Confederate surgeon who visited Andersonville in August 1864, testified that the brook was insufficient to wash away fecal matter, leaving "a mass of liquid excrement" over the swampy terrain around it. As the men developed dysentery from their diet, "The low grounds bordering the stream were covered with human excrements and filth of all kinds, which in many places seemed to be alive with working maggots. An indescribable sickening stench arose from these fermenting masses of human filth." This unspeakable pollution was the main source of drinking water for over 30,000 men.

The food consisted mainly of corn meal and bacon. Cooking facilities were so inadequate that half of the prison alternately received raw rations. The bacon was very salty, yellow, and maggoty, while the raw corn meal was unbolted, with the cob ground in, along with some sand and gravel. As the prisoners' digestive systems deteriorated from disease and malnutrition, this meal acted like broken glass on their stomachs and intestines.

To what extent was Captain Wirz responsible for these conditions? He had no hand in the location or construction of the stockade and was not assigned to duty there until the end of March 1864. Heinrich Hartmann Wirz was Swiss, born in 1823 in Zurich. He attended school in Zurich and Italy. After his first wife divorced him, he came in 1849 to the United States, where he remarried. When the war began, he was practicing medicine on a Louisiana plantation. Wirz enlisted as a private in the 4th Louisiana Infantry but was soon promoted to sergeant because of military training in Europe. At the Battle of Seven Pines on May 31–June 1, 1862, he received crippling and extremely painful wounds in the right shoulder and above the right wrist. These never healed; his right arm was almost useless. In June he was promoted to captain and made assistant adjutant general commanding the military prisons in Richmond. Wirz spent 1863 in Europe as special

Andersonville Prison, south view. The wagon in the fore-ground is labeled "Dead 12,877." In the right foreground an escaped prisoner is being attacked by hounds. This sketch by John B. Walker was published by T. Sinclair's in 1865.(LC)

agent of Jefferson Davis. A month after his return to the Confederacy he was commandant of the interior prison at Andersonville under John H. Winder, Commissary General of Prisons.

At first, rations improved under Wirz, but not for long. By mid-April 1864 the quality and quantity were becoming steadily worse. Wirz did appeal to General Winder for more rations, but when they were not forthcoming he refused both to let farmers and their wives bring in donations of food for the suffering men, nor would he allow his sentries or prisoners under guard out into the countryside to forage for rations. Though Wirz's defenders claimed that the prisoners had rations comparable to those of Confederate soldiers, the men in gray were not starving. When Major General William T. Sherman's army marched through Georgia, they "found abundance of corn, molasses, meal, bacon and sweet potatoes," plus much livestock and poultry. Wirz, however, refused to go beyond the limit of his orders, no matter what suffering resulted.

Nevertheless, when Major Thomas P. Turner inspected Andersonville on May 25, 1864, though he reported "gross mismanagement and want of system," he stated that Wirz "deserves great credit for the good sense and energy he has displayed. . . . He is the only man who seems to fully comprehend his important duties." Likewise, Lieutenant Colonel Daniel T. Chandler, sent from Richmond in August to inspect the prison, stated that "Capt. Henry Wirz . . . is entitled to commendation for his untiring energy and devotion to the discharge of the multifarious duties of this position, for which he is preeminently qualified."

Yet both Turner and Chandler found Andersville a horror almost beyond description. One clear villain, according to Confederates and Federals alike, was Wirz's commander, General Winder, who was repeatedly heard to boast that "I am killing off more Yankees than twenty regiments in Lee's Army." Yet Wirz could have taken more initiative, even without instructions from Winder. Dr. T. S. Hopkins, acting assistant surgeon at the prison, testified that Winder never visited Andersonville during the summer of 1864 and that Wirz had pretty much a free hand; he could have paroled prisoners, provided firewood, erected barracks, dug wells, and put a wooden floor under the hospital tents. He did enlarge the stockade once, but he could have further expanded it to relieve crowding. In his defense, Wirz insisted that he was not authorized to take any of these actions. Hopkins insisted Wirz could have carried out the recommendations without much trouble.

Instead, Wirz did nothing, and the result was starvation, but not immediately. By the time of death, most corpses were emaciated from the slow progress of disease. First came chronic dysentery, violent diarrhea that left the men shudder-

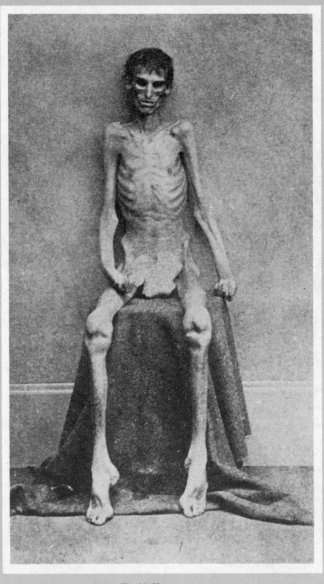

A victim of Andersonville. (LC)

ing with agonizing intestinal cramps. Soon came scurvy from lack of Vitamin C. It appeared first in the mouth, causing rot and bleeding in the gums and "spreading ulcers covered with a dark, purplish fungus growth." Dr. Joseph Jones testified that the parotid glands were sometimes swollen so that victims could not speak. Teeth fell out and gums broke off in bloody fragments. Dr. William Balser of South Carolina testified that scurvy caused necrosis of the jaws and that he had to extract pieces of jawbone nearly an inch long. The disease made gangrenous scorbutic ulcers break out all over the body; in them maggots laid their eggs. Limbs became soft and swollen, and blood became so impure that gangrene would set in at the slightest abrasion of the skin. Some prisoners went completely blind from ulceration of the anterior portion of the cornea. Scurvy also caused the leg tendons to draw up in cramped contortions so that the victim could not walk. Daubed with their own feces, the prisoners were swarming with vermin and worms feeding on the running sores. Boston Corbett, who later claimed to have shot John Wilkes Booth, was a prisoner at Andersonville, and he testified at the trial that "there were maggots there a foot deep or more"; when the rags were removed from one dead man, "the lice seemed as thick as the garment—a living mass."

While some prisoners wasted away to living skeletons, others became swollen and bloated with dropsy. Some suffered from bronchitis, consumption, pneumonia, erysipelas, and general lassitude, or a combination of them. When smallpox broke out, the men were vaccinated with an impure virus which caused further gangrene. Some arms rotted almost in two, and S. M. Dufur observed that "It was nothing strange to see a man who had been vaccinated six months, with his arm half or two-thirds eaten off, the bare cords exposed to view, and only dry, dark colored skin covering the bone." The prosecution charged that Wirz deliberately had impure vaccine administered in order to kill prisoners.

But Wirz's sins were not all those of omission. As prison commandant, he had the simultaneous responsibility of keeping the prisoners alive and preventing them from escaping. A petty and ineffectual bureaucrat, he seems to have been overwhelmed by the task of keeping order and so became obsessed by the one thing he could do—prevent escapes and punish those who attempted them. He therefore strictly enforced the dead line. Dozens of witnesses swore that men who dared reach beyond it for a stick of wood or a cup of purer water were shot, under Wirz's orders. Guards sometimes shot prisoners for merely putting their hands on the dead line to steady themselves. The prisoners insisted that guards told them Wirz gave a thirty-day furlough for every man they shot, but that may have been a story concocted by the guards to bully prisoners. Other issues aside, it was unlikely that Wirz could spare guards for so long. Certainly the charges were hearsay, and Confederate private Nazareth Allen said

General Lew Wallace made this sketch of The Dead Line *during the Andersonville trial. (Indiana Historical Society)*

The officers' stockade at Andersonville. Confederate hospitals and guards' barracks and camps appear in the distance.

he never heard Wirz promise to reward any guard who shot men crossing the dead line. He did hear the commander curse men and threaten to shoot them. Dozens of prisoners testified as to Wirz's cursing the men obscenely, in paroxysms of screaming rage, and threatening them with his revolver. Even Wirz himself admitted this. He struck and kicked those who merely broke rank at roll calls, and he repeatedly threatened to shoot them himself.

But did he ever pull the trigger? Numerous witnesses testified that they personally saw Wirz shoot someone, but they did not know the victim and could not give his name or regiment. Others were equally vague in insisting that they were present when Wirz ordered sentries to shoot prisoners who violated the dead line. Yet others reported that they did not see the actual killings but heard of them. Charles E. Tibbles testified, "I never saw a man shot there, but I heard the guns go off and saw the smoke, and saw the men after they were dead."

For the defense Baker challenged such evidence as hearsay, but repeatedly Wallace admitted it over Baker's objection. After Thomas Hall of the Marine Corps testified that he knew of various prisoners shot, Baker's cross examination made Hall concede, "I never saw Captain Wirz shoot a man. I never saw a man who was shot by him." Wallace then instructed the judge advocate "that it is very desirable to con-nect the circumstances that are testified to with the charges and specifications more specifically than has already been done."

> *The Judge Advocate.* Time and place are about the only particulars that can be testified to by these witnesses. They do not recollect names, and some of them hardly remember dates.
> *Mr. Baker.* They do not even remember the months.
> *The Judge Advocate.* I doubt whether you or I would remember anything if we had gone through what they have.
> *Mr. Baker.* Then you should not attempt to prove it.

When Wallace continued admitting hearsay evidence over Baker's objection, Baker and Schade announced on August 27 that it was their duty to withdraw from the case.

Wallace did not charge Baker and Schade with contempt of court, and two days later he readmitted them after Wirz wrote Chipman pleading that they be allowed again to represent him. Wallace replied, "Desirous of extending to the prisoner every consistent means of defence, the commission waive all personal objection to the attorneys named, and consent to their reappearance."

Animosity continued, but they stuck with the case. Baker complained that witnesses for the defense were bullied by the prosecution, so that many of them testified as the prosecution desired in order to be in good standing with the government. Questionable witnesses were those who told of Wirz's personally killing or ordering the death of prisoners. They accused him of thirteen distinct acts of murder; three by shooting with his own hand, one by stamping on a prisoner, three by torture in the stocks and chain gang, four by ordering sentries to fire upon prisoners, one by having a soldier torn in pieces by dogs, and one by beating a soldier with a revolver. The defense objected not only to hearsay testimony but to inconsistencies in dates and details and to general vagueness.

Witnesses were often vague about dates by as much as several months. Naturally, they would be uncertain as to exact days, as they had no accurate way of keeping a calendar. But sometimes Chipman changed the specifications to fit the testimony. When the defense proved that Wirz was absent from Andersonville from August 4 to 20, one charge of murder had its date changed to August 25. Only one witness gave the name, rank, and regiment of a man Wirz supposedly murdered, in the middle of September. None of the thirteen specifications charged murder at that time, so the court revised a charge from June 13 to a September date. George W. Gray of the 7th Indiana Cavalry testified that Wirz then personally killed William Stewart, private of the 9th Minnesota Infantry. Gray was an unsavory character, an admitted former slave catcher, who when asked how he knew about bloodhounds, boasted that he used to use them to hunt slaves in Virginia, where he had "real good sport" and "a good deal of fun catching niggers." Critics have suggested that Gray was a perjured witness hired by the prosecution, but there is no proof of this. One of the most damaging witnesses for the prosecution, Felix de la Baume, who said he saw Wirz shoot and wound two men, one of whom he later heard had died, was afterward proved to be Felix Oeser, a deserter whose reliability was accordingly suspect.

Two cases to which Wirz conceded some validity were those of "Frenchy" and "Chickamauga." Numerous prisoners insisted that Wirz had a prisoner known as Frenchy killed by dogs when he tried to escape. Wirz admitted that there was a Frenchy who repeatedly tried to escape but insisted that when Frenchy fell out of a tree and dogs rushed him, Wirz drove the beasts off and then had the prisoner exchanged at the first opportunity.

More damaging was the case of Chickamauga. Fourteen prisoners testified in remarkably consistent detail that Chickamauga, a feeble-minded, one-legged cripple, deliberately crossed the dead line, insisting he would rather be shot than stay in the stockade, and that he begged the guard to kill him. When the guard refused, Wirz called over a sentry and ordered him to tell the prisoner to go back over the dead line and to shoot him if he did not. When Chickamauga refused

to move, the sentry shot him in the jaw and through the breast. Wirz admitted the episode but questioned the interpretation. He claimed that when the prisoner caused a disturbance, "I went up to 'Chickamauga' and asked him in a rough tone of voice, what the hell he was doing there. He said he wanted to be killed. I took my revolver in my hand and said, in a menacing manner, that if that was all he wanted I would accommodate him. I scared him somewhat, and he was taken outside by some of the prisoners. I then, in his presence, and solely as a menace, told the sentry to shoot him if he came in again." Wirz said he did not think that Chickamauga would return or that his comrades would let him, but as he was riding home from the stockade, he heard the shot.

Frederick Guscetti, a prisoner who saw the shooting of Chickamauga, testified for the defense that he could not hear what orders Wirz gave inside the sentry box. Having been personally well-treated by Wirz, Guscetti signed a letter soliciting funds for his defense. Baker objected to Chipman's cross-examining Guscetti on this letter, since "I was held to the strict rule that I could not cross-examine on any subject that was not touched in the direct examination." Chipman replied, "I want to discredit this witness in any way I can." On another occasion, objecting to Chipman's attempt to challenge the credibility of a witness for the defense, Baker said he never did so to those of the prosecution, "who, the court knows, were open to reflections of that kind." In response, Chipman admitted the court's bias: "The gentleman does not seem to understand the status of witnesses.... The gentleman says he did not attack the credibility of the rebel witnesses, and therefore the government must not do it; whereas the gentleman knows very well that the presumption is that those

(continued)

Hut where hounds and a bull terrier were kept for pursuit of escaping prisoners. Witnesses at Wirz's trial testified that some were killed by the dogs. (KA)

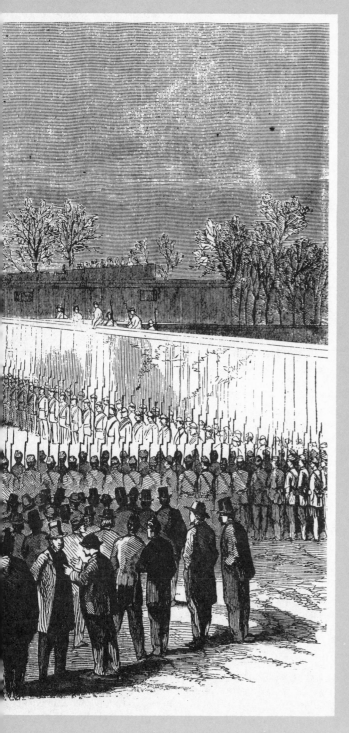

The execution of Captain Wirz, November 10, 1865, in the Washington Arsenal where the Lincoln conspirators had been hanged four months earlier.

Wirz is depicted in this magazine illustration being dressed for execution in black robe and hood. (FL)

(continued)

who were in sympathy with the South, were also in sympathy with this defendant."

The prosecution's strongest case was against Wirz's causing the death of prisoners in the stocks and chain gang. For attempting to escape or for mere insubordination, Wirz had men flogged, bucked, and put in the standing stocks, sometimes suspended with only their toes touching the ground. Joseph Achuff testified that Wirz kept him in the stocks under a broiling sun with no food for thirty-six hours, after which he was put in irons, which ate into his legs. Others within the stockade were put in chain gangs—a deadly punishment, considering their enfeebled condition. As many as twelve were chained together in a circle by the neck, with chains extending from their iron collars to handcuffs, to chains on their feet, which were also connected in a circle and attached to thirty-two and sixty-four pound balls. Some were kept chained all day for weeks. Like Siamese twins, all had to move together, blistered by the sun and tortured by dysentery. Many died as a result.

Whether intentional or not, Andersonville was a crime against humanity, and Wirz was made to pay for it. More than one-fourth of the prisoners died: 12,920 fatalities out of approximately 45,000 men imprisoned there. Untold others were crippled, mutilated, or diseased for life. But was Wirz alone to blame? General John H. Winder was more responsible for the inadequate rations and facilities, but Winder was dead and beyond legal vengeance. Certainly other prisons on both sides in the war had inhumane conditions. While 15.5 percent of Union prisoners died in Confederate camps, a little more than 12 percent of Confederates died in such Northern prisons as Fort Delaware, Camp Douglas, Rock Island, and Elmira, New York. At Elmira, a fourth of the prisoners suffered scurvy. These horrors were no more intentional than Andersonville, although Senator Ben Wade did introduce resolutions in the Senate to retaliate for Andersonville by deliberately starving and freezing Confederates in Federal prisons.

But Chipman insisted that Union violations did not justify Confederate atrocities. He refused to subpoena witnesses who would testify to conditions in Union prisons. The defense subpoenaed the Confederate commissioner for the exchange of prisoners to testify to the effect of the Union's ending the prisoner exchange program, but Chipman made him surrender his subpoena and prevented him from testifying. Wirz thus became a symbolic victim. In October the trial was temporarily adjourned when Wirz became ill, but Wallace was determined to bring things to a conclusion and ordered Wirz to be carried into court on a stretcher. In the courtroom, he reclined on a chaise longue, which seemed to symbolize his helpless vulnerability.

When they were not allowed two weeks to prepare their final statement for the defense, Schade and Baker withdrew from the case altogether, leaving Wirz to summarize his own defense. He never took the stand himself but had a long statement read, full of bitter sarcasm, in which he tried once more to prove that he had done all that circumstances permitted and that he was not responsible for the orders he obeyed. He did admit that he put prisoners in the stocks and chain gangs but said he was not aware that such punishments "are unusual or cruel."

Summing up the case for the prosecution on October 20, Chipman spent seven pages trying to justify the jurisdiction of the military tribunal. The case was without specific precedent, and Chipman apparently felt himself on shaky ground, to protest so much.

Chipman could find no precedent for a military commission's trying a soldier of a foreign army, but he cited precedents for their trying civilians during the Revolution, the Whiskey Insurrection, the Burr conspiracy, and other occasions. By his logic, the Wirz case was unique. Chipman would not admit that the Confederacy was a foreign nation. Therefore, Wirz was not the officer of a foreign army but a United States civilian engaging in treasonable rebellion. Thus, if he should be tried, who could try him? The Confederate Government could and would not, and Chipman asserted without substantiation that no civil tribunal had the power to do so; thus only a military commission was left. Besides, he argued in inflammatory language, the war was not over; "by far the largest portion [of the Rebels] sullen, silent, vengeful, stand ready to seize every opportunity to divide the loyal sentiment of the country and with spirit unbroken and defiant, would this day raise the standard of rebellion if they dared hope for success." Chipman concluded that by the mere fact of constituting the court, President Johnson "declared the presence of a public danger. . . ."

After his lengthy defense of the jurisdiction of the court, Chipman took two more pages to answer Wirz's charges of unfair procedure, admitting to some. However, it is hardly believable that more than 100 witnesses from both armies would perjure themselves. Furthermore their testimony is reinforced by numerous diaries and memoirs of Andersonville prisoners who never appeared at the trial.

On October 24, after sixty-three days, the trial closed. Wirz was found guilty on one charge of conspiracy and on eleven out of thirteen specifications of murder, "two thirds of the members of the court concurring therein." Wallace wrote a summary of the findings and pronounced sentence of death. Judge Advocate General Joseph Holt reviewed the trial and found no fault. The New York *World* disagreed, charging that "The extraordinary conduct of the court. . . tends to create an impression that they fear the prisoner might escape if they were to permit a vigorous cross-examination of the witnesses against him."

Wallace's summary and Holt's review were forwarded to President Johnson, who approved the court's findings, upheld the sentence, and set November 10 for the hanging. The Catholic priest who attended Wirz during the interval of waiting and on the scaffold, later maintained that Wirz was offered a pardon if he would implicate Jefferson Davis in the Andersonville atrocities and that Wirz refused.

The government issued 250 spectators' tickets for the execution in the same prison yard at the arsenal grounds where the Lincoln conspirators had been hanged four months earlier. Others, morbidly curious, competed for perches in the elm trees and on nearby rooftops overlooking the walls. Surrounded by four companies of soldiers chanting, "Wirz, remember Andersonville," the prisoner told the commanding officer, "I know what orders are, Major. And I am being hanged for obeying them." At 10:32 the trap was sprung. The fall did not break Wirz's neck, and his legs continued to writhe within their bonds as he slowly strangled, while the chanting continued, "Wirz, remember Andersonville."

The judgment is still being challenged. Anti-administration newspapers immediately declared that Wirz was tried unfairly and punished unjustly. The Confederates in turn hailed Wirz as a hero. Jefferson Davis wrote that Wirz "died a martyr to a cause through adherence to truth." The Georgia Chapter of the United Daughters of the Confederacy charged that Wirz was "judicially murdered" and in 1909 erected a monument to him, naming him a "hero-martyr" and quoting Grant's refusal to exchange prisoners. Otis Baker called Wirz "the bravest man I ever saw."

But one might find much greater courage in the endurance, dignity, and indomitable will that enabled some prisoners to survive far more suffering than Wirz. It is at least ironic justice that Henry Wirz was the last victim of Andersonville.

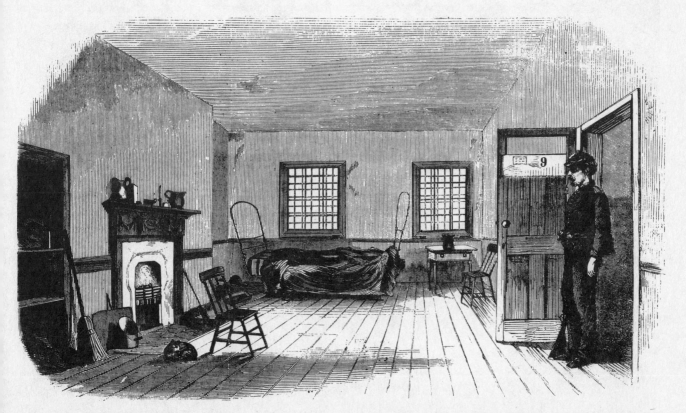

A sketch by Frank H. Schell was the source for a magazine illustration showing the interior of Wirz's room in Old Capitol Prison. (FL)

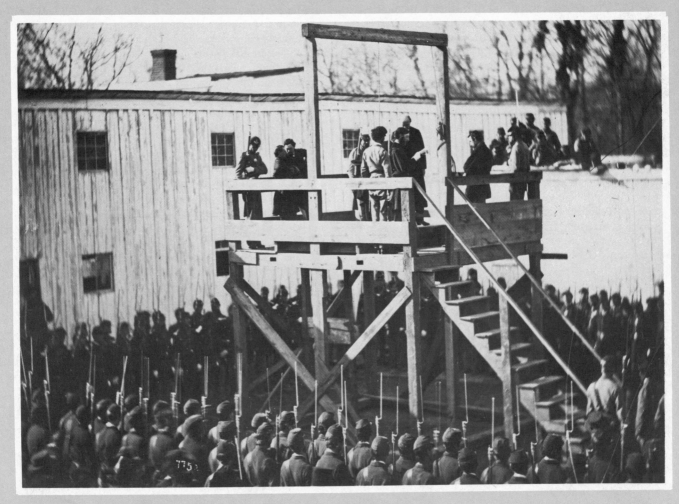

The execution of Wirz. The noose is adjusted as a Catholic priest stands by. (LC)

The trap is sprung. With neck unbroken in the fall, Wirz writhed in his death throes. (LC)

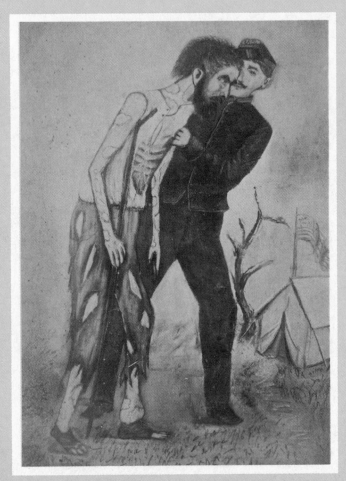

McIntosh as he appeared upon his release from Andersonville.

Patronize an Old "Vet"

These two unusual pictures were submitted by Arthur S. Howard, Scottsdale, Arizona. They are reproductions of two cards offered for sale to the public by E. W. McIntosh, who apparently supported himself after the war by traveling with a guitar and playing his own song, "Dixie's Sunny Land." The message contained on the reverse side of the card depicting McIntosh as a survivor of Andersonville details the old soldier's life and war record:

This photo [actually a drawing] is a copy of the original, taken from a tin type, by a rebel artist at parole camp near Vicksburg, March 28th 1865; it is a correct photo of E. W. McIntosh, of Co. E. 14th Illinois Infantry, as he appeared after having been confined at Andersonville prison from October 4th 1864 until March 28, 1865. He enlisted at Bloomington, and was mustered in at Jacksonville, Illinois, May 25th, 1861. When captured by the Rebs, at Ackworth, Ga., his weight was 175 pounds, when exchanged he was reduced to 65 pounds, and almost destitute of clothing. Through intense suffering and starvation, he became afflicted with spinal disease, causing mental derangement which incapacitates him for either mental or physical labor. Scurvey also entered his system, causing gangreenous sores to almost cover his body. He is one of the survivors of the fatal steamer Sultana, which was blown up on the Mississippi river April 27th 1865, and was in the water until the afternoon when he was rescued by some colored men and taken to Overton hospital, Memphis, Tenn. He was discharged at Springfield, Ill., June 30th, 1865, and has been under the doctor's care ever since. He now travels for his health and sells his photo to defray expenses. Every citizen ought to buy one, not only to help the old "Vet" along, but also to show the rising generation what it cost to purchase the freedom they enjoy to-day. He also sells his song with music, "Dixie's Sunny Land," which he composed while in the rebel prison pen. Patronize the old soldier that he may go on his way. This photo and song, 25 cents each, or both for 40 cents.

McIntosh after the war, on the road with his guitar.

Some of the nearly 13,000 graves of Union soldiers who died at Andersonville. After the war the dead were reburied at the site in a National Cemetery.